Worlds of Experience:
Communities in Colonial Virginia

Detail from the Fry-Jefferson Map showing the pattern of settlement in tidewater Virginia.

The Foundations of America

Worlds of Experience: Communities in Colonial Virginia

By Rhys Isaac

The Colonial Williamsburg Foundation
Williamsburg, Virginia

The publication of this book is made possible through a gift from Kathe and John Dyson.

It is April 1776. This is the time when Virginia and the united colonies are still anxiously deciding whether or not to declare themselves independent and become the United States. A report of a happy accident reaches Williamsburg from across the York River. At the Gloucester County Courthouse the gentlemen justices had been seated on their raised bench ready to begin their monthly session. But first there was an opening procedure in which the sheriff spoke some customary words used for starting a colonial court held in the king's name. Virginia's Seventh Regiment was camped outside on the courthouse green—hundreds of men were there in arms against the king's administration. Inside, the sheriff was going to conclude the little ceremony with the usual pronouncement, "God Save the King," when (so the report ran) "just as he was about pronouncing the words, a *five's* ball, struck by a soldier of the 7th regiment (playing handball), entered the window, and knocked him in the mouth, which prevented him from being guilty of so much impiety." At least that was what the patriotic writer of the newspaper story concluded!

The Gloucester County Courthouse was a typical mustering place for local units of the army that ended the king of England's reign in America.

This little incident is an amusing miniature of a very serious aspect of the American Revolution. The flying handball had certainly given the sheriff of Gloucester County a sharp jolt out of his old ways and his habitual colonial loyalty to the king, but most persons experienced only a little less abruptly the turn-around that came with choosing independence and learning to be part of a separate nation. It is important for us to try to understand the world that these colonial Americans were leaving behind when they made this break, and to consider the changes they were experiencing as they committed themselves to establishing and sustaining the new United States.

Understanding the past is always difficult and there are many ways to approach it. Let's attempt a bold and challenging one suited to the present age and to the media through which we now pick up much of the history that we carry about with us—film and television. Suppose we were not watching a screen but were ourselves putting together a videotape about colonial Virginia as it approached the Revolution. Perhaps we would want to include the scene just described. What would we have to know to be able to make it truly live again? Obviously we'd have to learn a lot in detail about costume, buildings, and furniture styles—the familiar kinds of authenticity in museum and historical feature film presentations. But wouldn't we also have to know the people and how they were different from us in attitude and in the kinds of behavior they expected from each other? In a word, wouldn't we have to get to know *their* world as *they* knew it?

Getting to know people ultimately involves us in understanding their responses and having an appreciation of their values—that is, sensing what really matters to them and what it means. A film that is going to bring us close to the colonial world and the actions of those who participated in the Revolution would have to seek out the daily life circumstances of the people of the time. It would need to begin with a survey of the whole society to reveal the different kinds of community there were in it, then it would have to move in close to discover the ways of those communities—the formative life experiences they offered—and finally to explore ways in which those past communities were linked and organized together.

Gaining that kind of understanding will come partly from learning about life stories, childhood experiences, and everyday circumstances. We sense how all these have made and continue to make a person what he or she is. But we should not look to find these persons growing up in a static world. Virginia, like all America then, was a changing place. Those who came of age there in the mid-eighteenth century gained their knowledge of life in a society that was experiencing problems of adjustment that eventually led to a world-shaking revolution. Not only the colonists' political system but their religion and their ways of thinking about themselves and their communities were profoundly altered before that generation had given way to the next. A search for understanding of colonial times must include a view of the trends that were, subtly at first, and then boldly and dramatically, revolutionizing people's ways of being. The changes reveal an increasing emphasis on individuals, their privacy, their rights, and their salvation. Consideration of these developments will also help us to comprehend something of how we got "here" from "there," that is, to understand how the processes of the past have created the present that confronts us.

Kinds of Community

A film can very easily include an overview. If we take a camera up fifteen or twenty thousand feet in the air, we can see the whole of tidewater and piedmont Virginia—the settled region of colonial times—spread out below us. We can see the natural features that made the Old Dominion what it was: the

Cities and the highways that connect them are now the main features of the map of Virginia.

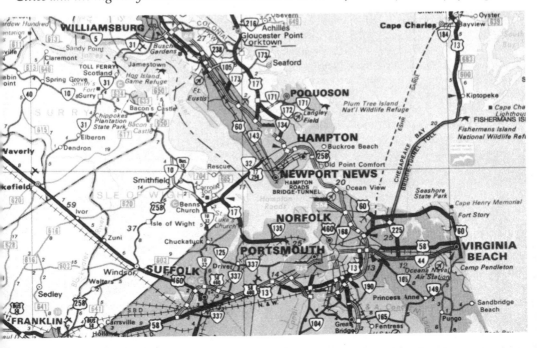

swamps and the abundance of timber, and, most important, Chesapeake Bay and the rivers opening into it—so many arms and fingers of the sea that are able to carry maritime commerce far inland. But how much is different from what our camera picks up now if we could have flown over the same area two hundred years ago?

A map is a way of seeing the surface of the earth from thousands of feet up—a way invented long before the camera and the airplane. In 1754 a map of Virginia was published by Colonels Joshua Fry and Peter Jefferson, father of the later president. The most striking difference between the Virginia of our present-day aerial photograph and the map of 1754 is the entire absence of cities in the earlier overview. The smallest towns of modern Virginia would be bigger than the largest settlements shown on the old map. The least important modern town would dwarf the Williamsburg or Norfolk of colonial times.

Mountains and rivers were the main features on this eighteenth-century map of Virginia. Most of the places named were not towns but great family plantations.

By the time of the Revolution there are some four hundred thousand people in Virginia, most of whom live in the tidewater and piedmont regions east of the Blue Ridge. There are about two hundred forty thousand free whites, and one hundred sixty thousand blacks, who are nearly all slaves. Where would we find them? The other great difference between an aerial view then and now would give an indication of that. There is much less forest, since more of the land in the tidewater region is cleared and appears either as planted fields or as old fields abandoned for a time until their fertility returns. Nearly all of the people live among those fields, removing or thinning out the trees relentlessly with their constant demands for land, for building and fencing materials, and for firewood.

The way places are marked on the Fry-Jefferson map gives a clue as to how all this work is distributed and controlled. If we disregard the names attached to natural features like creeks and swamps, most of the placenames turn out to be family surnames, and they make a kind of fishbone pattern as they are

Nearly all colonial Virginians lived on small farms or at slave quarters scattered among the fields and woods. Courtesy, University of North Carolina Press.

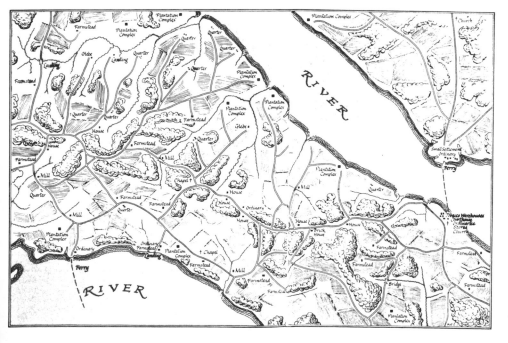

5

shown on the map, written out sideways from the rivers. The settlements marked are the plantations of the great families who have located themselves along the inland waterways at places where ships could load and unload. They thus dominate commerce and communications in their world—just as their names dominate its maps.

But these powerful families make up less than ten percent of the population. Where are the rest? A single set of early maps prepared by artillerymen for the siege of Yorktown shows where our camera can pick up the more than ninety percent of the people whose labor supports the small proportion of fine gentlefolk. They are either clustered in "quarters" if they are blacks, or are scattered on small farms if they are whites.

The scale of everyday community in this colonial world is very small indeed since most people live and work in the little setting of a quarter or a one-family plantation. (All colonial Virginia farms whether great or small were called plantations in the eighteenth century.) Our aerial camera zooming in on the activities at and around the dwelling places shows us how gainful employment and domestic life are not separated as in our own urbanized world. We see that children grow up laboring alongside brothers and sisters under their parents' command. Among whites the owner of a farm, an artisan workshop, or a plantation, even if he is no sort of kin to his workers, thinks of himself as a kind of father who exercises a paternal authority over all persons on his place.

Since individual equality is not even an ideal in the colonial world, and fathers are expected to be stern and demanding, their combining the role of parent with that of employer does not mean that everyone is treated alike or anyone is treated gently. Even the word family then meant, not our idea of a close, supposedly cosy domestic circle, but a work force that could be as big as that of a great plantation and still be described as "the whole family black and white." The heads of such households thought of themselves as patriarchs like Abraham in the Bible, with his "Flocks and . . . Herds, . . . Bond-men and Bond-women" (that is, slaves). Indeed, it is we who have changed this meaning of the word family in accordance with our modern ideas; originally it came from the Latin word *famulus*, a servant.

Filmmakers wanting to communicate the authentic feel of daily life in colonial Virginia have to imagine ways to capture the closeness of these living and working together households.

Plantation communities have to be shown in such a way that we sense how the mutual involvement of the inhabitants of these small worlds increases rather than diminishes their awareness of difference and inequality. In this exploration we must try to adopt one of the most important presentation devices of the cinema—the set of camera techniques whereby we are made to feel we see through another's eyes. Since we need to know the close worlds of the quarter, the family farm plantation, and the Virginia gentleman's great house as their inhabitants knew them, we cannot do better than to try to follow some of the main learning experiences of a young person raised in each of these settings.

The Slave Quarter

Black children growing up on a colonial plantation had been born into settlements we can recognize as little Afro-American villages that were called quarters. Let us first follow the learning experiences of a little black girl named Filis. The name is chosen because it expresses the divided experience of slaves; the white people assumed it to be the English name "Phyllis," though it was not one they used much themselves. In fact, it probably came from the African name "Fili," denoting the day of the child's birth.

Our camera shows the settlement at the quarter where the little girl began her life. It is made up of a number of one-room dwellings, each sixteen feet by sixteen or less. Perhaps there is a slightly larger barrack of sixteen feet by twenty housing workers who are not married or whose husbands or wives live on another plantation. Smallness of space impresses us as we pan around the inside of one of these huts or cabins. From the start, domestic life for Filis is a close, physically intimate experience. This closeness belongs not only to the family's particular living space. All the dwellings are very near together. Their inhabitants share a yard and other facilities; they live in a communal cluster that has no equivalent in the white people's world. (Among the whites, each married pair lives on an isolated farm, since they are determined, as one explains it, to "keep troublesome neighbors at a distance.")

Inside the dwellings at the slaves' quarter we see the furnishings. Beds are heaps of straw, seats are upturned barrels. The only equipment the master supplies are pots, perhaps a handmill or grindstone for turning corn into meal for the staple

Part of this old slave house dates from the eighteenth century. Much of the living occurred in the communal yard.

pone, and the hoes and axes needed for plantation work and for tending the gardens around the quarter where slaves raise vegetable provisions to supplement their rations. The standard rations are two gallons of corn per adult per week, plus amounts of fish and meat that vary according to the master's degree of meanness.

While Filis lives with both her mother and her father, not all the other children at the quarter are so fortunate. Half the children grow up at a distance from fathers who are forced to live at another quarter or even on another plantation. Early in her life, Filis watches the selling away of playmates, some of them as young as two years old when this severance takes place. We see how relationships in Filis's little world are shaped by the regulation of the slaves' time. From the start all the mothers are kept many hours from the infants. They are allowed time off from arduous field work only three times in the long day to suckle their little ones. Once weaned, we see how the child is left at the quarter in the care of a slave too old to work, assisted by a nine-year-old girl. As she grows up, Filis performs similar services. Gradually, as she increases in strength, she has to undertake more and more of the labors of raising crops. This toil will continue for the rest of her life.

Let us now close in on that little cluster of cabins with their straw beds, iron pots, and gourd utensils and their small, dark, smoke-blackened interiors. Slavery was a poisonous evil; it denied the inhabitants of the quarter even the right to bring up their own children and to be cared for by them in old age; it was a system that held the whip always at the slaves' backs. That oppression must not be forgotten, but we can best acknowledge the slaves' own humanity by resisting our impulse to define them merely as victims.

Our scanning, interpreting camera shows viewers how to see the creative adaptations achieved at the quarter, how to recognize in that collection of huts, and in those crowded, scarcely furnished rooms, not simply deprivation, not just our modern way of life destructively compressed, but a *very different way*. Today's middle-class values are shared by most Americans whether black or white. We depend on a great range of material possessions, and we use them, whether they be the rooms of our houses or the enclosing shapes of easy chairs, to separate even members of our own family from ourselves. We take a right to personal space and privacy for granted. Those who grew up and lived on a Virginia slave quarter came from a different, African tradition that used architecture and furniture to keep individuals in close physical contact with each other. Privacy was not even an ideal; on the contrary, those reared in this world found their greatest rewards in shared collective feelings.

Filis is learning from this setting to know the world in a certain way. The life of the quarter, and the way the people arrange and occupy their living space, teach her important lessons: she understands the respect due to age from the fact that the foremost place is accorded to the older man who is the leader and foreman of work; she learns the enduring importance of kinship ties from the supportive relationships that brothers and sisters continue to have toward each other and toward each other's children throughout their adult lives; and she learns a sense of inclusive community from the very layout of the place. The close proximity and togetherness intermingles the lives of each cabin's occupants with those in all the dwellings of the quarter so that they share the business of child rearing and other daily tasks.

There are also the lessons openly taught in the vibrant activities of the little settlement. Today's materialistic, middle-class society has made a fetish of books as the core of knowledge. The ways of Filis's community lead her to kinds of knowledge that exist in the living, collectively created experiences of song, dance, and storytelling—vital parts of an ensemble we call oral culture. This is summed up in a number of traditional forms, some of which later will come to be written down as spirituals. A song is not a fixed set of words but a number of themes familiar to all the members of the society.

Growing up in the slave quarter meant learning about the world through close community experiences.

Our camera moves us in among a group of slaves and shows how, when the mood is ripe, a leader can either revive or make up a line and have all the others join in a call-and-response communal performance. We see from a series of variations how each performance refashions the song, expressing immediately shared concerns. Seeing the faces of the participants and sensing in the sound the quality of feelings that unites them, we become aware of how such collective performances produce a set of life experiences very different from anything we can readily imagine.

Thus Filis learns of herself as part of a different people who have a knowledge of mankind—and of God and all things—that the white masters cannot have. Following the child's participation, we begin to learn how her people's Afro-American songs, their seemingly cynical animal trickster tales, and their herbal lore speak to Filis of a deeply felt connectedness of human society with the whole of creation. We see her learning to conduct herself properly toward the omnipresent spirit world. Like her own life, that world is full of dangers to be averted, but there are also ways to insure safety in all things for those who learn how to manage.

The songs and dances often teach about the ways slaves must expect to be treated by their masters or mistresses; often they mock those powerful white folk whose weaknesses are so well known. The repertoire of tales contains a rich and varied store of recipes for survival. There are both moral tales (little known to whites) and trickster tales (of which the Brer Rabbit collections form only a small part). All of them teach priorities and ways to survive.

Cutting between storytelling, commentary, and situations, our film shows the many applications of the wisdom stored in the folktales. Taken together, they make up a diagram of human nature with all its greedy demands, frauds, and cruelties—a diagram of human nature regardless of race. Close observation reveals how the stories are also a means to reverse oppression by showing how the enslaved may triumph. We see the satirical sketches of the society of the powerful whites—they appear as animal characters who have no work to do but are free to manipulate others. Those young slaves who are sold away very early from their parents certainly need such knowledge to prepare them for the hardships of a life in which the masters harshly control where and with whom they live, as well as demanding long hours of arduous toil six days a week.

At an early age young slaves began a lifetime of toil in the fields, often under the supervision of an overseer. Courtesy, Papers of Benjamin Henry Latrobe, Maryland Historical Society, Baltimore.

The outward aspects of labor in the fields are easily shown in film. The real challenge is to communicate how the demands of work and its seasonal rhythms contribute to the slaves' whole way of life. Filis is familiar from infancy with the raising of crops. As soon as she is strong enough, she is moved from tasks like child minding or sheep- and cowherding to a lifetime of tilling the fields. The swinging of a hoe, and the various tasks performed with it, is most of the action our camera will have to show.

The tobacco seedbeds must be hoed soft and ready in late winter. The ground in the tobacco and corn fields is broken up in the spring. All through March and April we see how the earth—often stiff clay—has to be heaped with special hoes into hills about a foot high, spaced at three-foot intervals in rows that are seven feet apart. When that is done, and as soon as a season (a spring shower of rain) makes conditions right, Filis with her elders is out in the muddy fields, bending over some six thousand times in a day to make holes with a finger or a stick in the crown of each hill and slip a tobacco seedling or three seeds of corn into the ground.

Once the corn and tobacco are growing, the same workers have the endless task of moving through the rows chopping the weeds. Watching, we can sense how all this drudgery is made more tolerable by the chants that unite the people as they labor, keeping the hoes swinging at a slow, even rate.

Yet we must beware and not fall for the comfortable stereotype of the happy darkies on the ole plantation. As the plants grow high, the tedious tasks of worming (removing caterpillars by hand) and topping (snipping off the central bud) call for further long hours in the sultry sun. Crop tending gives way by late August to the arduous operations of harvesting—cutting, stacking, and hanging the crop on stakes heavy with tobacco plants that have to be hoisted up high in the great tobacco houses. The next stage is indoor work—the stripping and tying of the moist, sweated sotweed leaves into bundles or hands. Since this work can be continued by firelight after sundown, we see how long the working hours become in the month after the harvest.

Winter brings some relief from field work, but, because America's climate was colder then than it is now, those slaves who have the task of supplying the grand white squire's household with logs are bringing in three wagonloads a day during the season. In a large plantation house there are as many as twenty-eight great open fires burning. For slaves themselves the gathering of firewood is an urgent matter of survival.

The Small Farm

In showing Filis's experiences of fieldwork, our film will already have given us glimpses of the white overseer. Indeed, since overseers usually stayed only a year or so, we will have seen the growing child meet a succession of such men, and through them get acquainted with another way of life, not quite as poor yet nearly as toilsome as her own. The overseer is a young man in his late teens or early twenties who lives in a little house close by the quarter. He comes from a small plantation background and is striving to make enough from wages and his share of the gentleman's crop to get stocked and started as a small planter on his own. Like the slaves, he has been used to hard work in the fields from an early age, since the sons of common planters are an important part of their fathers' work force. This is so even when the father has accumulated enough wealth to buy a slave or two to increase his crop production.

Following the overseer back from the fringe of the slave quarter right into his own world, our film now introduces us to a very different part of the colony's population. More aerial views, intercut with closeups of scenes in fields and small houses, show that hardhanded, field-working smallholders of English descent are the largest part (about fifty to sixty percent) of the whole population of colonial tidewater Virginia—although, by the 1770s in some counties in the Williamsburg region, black majorities have already appeared. The people of this class, whom our camera reveals going about their daily tasks, would today be called tobacco farmers, but, as we find them, they are called common planters. This description distinguishes them from the gentlefolk. (The name of gentleman was reserved for those who did not bend their backs in the fields and who lived free from all manual labor—the class whom we now refer to as planters.)

The aerial shots show Anglo-Virginian common planters living everywhere in one-family groupings. Unlike the slaves at the quarters, we find them separated by their fields, woodlands, and swamps from other families of their own kind. Their farms of a few hundred acres make patterns of cleared fields, abandoned fields, and areas partially reclaimed by forest. Before the days of fertilizers, fields became exhausted after only a few years' use. Also, farmers needed lots of wood for construction, packaging, and burning, so it was necessary to let fields grow again into woods every few years and to clear new land. Consequently, although each laborer could only work about three acres of tobacco, a farmer or planter needed about fifty

White "common planters," who made up the majority of colonial Virginians, lived in small houses on isolated farms.

acres for every working hand—one hundred fifty acres, then, for a smallholder who had two sons old enough to work his fields before they left him to set up on their own.

Our camera picks out and focuses on one smallholder's farm. At its heart is what was then called a Virginia house, together with its outbuildings. The house has a distinctive style; from close up it is seen to be framed with squared posts and beams, covered—roof and walls—with riven clapboards (that is, four-foot lengths of oak split with a blade called a froe). The dwellings are very small by our standards. A typical one measures only sixteen by twenty-one feet and has one or some-times two rooms downstairs with corresponding attics above. The chimney is not brick but wood lined with clay. The win-dows are without glass; wooden shutters keep out the weather.

The film, cutting back to views of Williamsburg and of the great plantation houses, reminds us that the dwellings in town (and at Mount Vernon, for example) are grand residences, and that the great majority of white folk live in cramped little cabins of much the same size and construction as the outbuildings in the yards of the Historic Area of Williamsburg.

Panning over the arrangement of the house and the out-houses and viewing the furnishings in them tells us more about the lives of their inhabitants than would a household survey in our urbanized age. We quickly sense how we, today, have separated work and domestic life while *they* experienced them

Indoor life and work took place in the same dark, crowded space.

15

together. We now have elaborate furniture and equipment to carry on our home lives; they then had only a few items of the simplest kind. Reflection on this tells us very eloquently how different from us their way of life must have made these plain folk of colonial times.

Accurate filmmaking is easier here. We do not have to guess at what to include in our review of a colonial farmer's stock of possessions; inventories prepared at the death of a householder listed every piece down to the cracked cup and the worn stockings. There was, of course, a range of inventories—from the small proportion that came from really poor free persons to the considerable number from middling households—but they all had only the most basic stocks. At the beginning of the eighteenth century the common folk had very little furniture in their one- or two-room houses. Their cooking utensils, frequently a single iron pot, confined their diet mainly to boiled foods.

Going back in time, our camera finds people eating, slouched on a chest or squatting against a wall. We are looking in on white farmers' houses that, like those of the slaves, have neither tables nor chairs. Chests for storage, and perhaps for sitting on, are the only items of furniture found in every home. The absence of candles and lamps in many cases reveals an important fact of the people's lives. Our film flashback must show firelight as the only illumination after dark. The number of blankets and beds is too small for the number of occupants, and so we see not only married couples but children and servants sleeping huddled body-to-body. The master and mistress are the only ones with a bedstead to raise them off the earthen floor. The others have only mattresses—a bag of cattails on the ground.

Moving forward again in time, we see that by the end of the colonial era common planters in better circumstances have acquired more of what we regard as the essentials for civilized living. Yet the stocks of household equipment are still very small by our standards. The greater part of the total of possessions are the working tools of the farm. Compared to the shortage of home comforts, we see a considerable collection of saws, hoes, axes, and corn grinders as well as livestock. These are the essentials in the struggle for subsistence.

We observe one of these farm families—five children and their parents who live in a little wooden-chimneyed Virginia house. They are working their fields in much the same ways the slaves do. They clear them from the forest with axes, cutting the trunks about three feet from the ground to prevent shooting from the base; they split the timber, making rails for the worm fences that enclose the fields and keep out the hogs and cattle. They too are forever hoeing as they hill the dirt between the standing stumps to be ready for the crops, and then as they fight against the choking growth of weeds. Corn and tobacco are the main supports of life for these folk. Corn is their bread, and tobacco is their money. We see the men bend their backs to their work, hardening their hands with the constant use of ax and hoe; the white womenfolk are, however, absent from the fields. They work hard, but in contrast to Filis and her black sisters, they work around the house and yard and seldom among the crops.

The lives of the small and middling farmers, or common planters, may also best be entered through following the experiences of a youngster growing up and learning to know the world. In this case, however, we have the memoirs of an actual farm boy to guide us. Devereux Jarratt was born in New Kent County in 1733. He was a third generation Virginian, the youngest son of a carpenter, who kept a farm as well. We can see the strong ideal of independence—and something of the homely realities—in Devereux's recollection that his parents had the "character of honesty and industry, by which they lived in credit among their neighbors, free from real want, and above the frowns of the world." (Poorer farmers were never clear of debts.) But the Jarratt family "always had plenty of plain food and raiment . . . suitable to their humble station." These supplies were "the produce of the farm, or plantation, except a little sugar, which was rarely used." He recalled also (perhaps exaggerating the degree of self-sufficiency) that "our raiment was altogether my mother's manufacture," except for the hats and shoes that were worn only "in the winter season."

We see how the little barefoot boy at an early age has already learned the inequalities, the rank structure, that define his lowly place in this social world. We see him confronted near his house by "a man riding the road," wearing a fine coat and the "periwig" that was then "a distinguishing badge of *gentle folk.*" He stares in awe for an instant, and then runs off, as for his life.

Observing more of his growing up, we see him acquire the kinds of knowledge appropriate to a boy of his rank. His parents, who are middling rather than poor folk, see to it that he learns "to read, write, and understand the fundamental rules of arithmetic." Even this much cannot be taken for granted, since there is no school system but in most parts only poor schoolmasters who set up where they can and take pupils for a small fee. Our film finds such a teacher in a little one-room building, struggling to pass on the rudiments of reading and writing to farm children who are more accustomed to tending crops than to turning pages, more used to wielding hoes than to holding pens. We see how the use of the Bible as the reading primer complicates the children's task, though it does, at the same time, teach a lesson about the sacred authority of learning and the printed word. Most of the girls among the pupils and many of the boys get even less of the three R's than young Jarratt.

Scripture, though usually interpreted through the prayer book of the established church, is part of the living culture of white colonial Virginians, but a strict and gloomy piety is not. Vigorous celebrations in dance, song, and sporting pastimes are also parts of that way of life. As with the child at the slave quarters, we follow the activities through which the young lad gains a particular kind of knowledge from participation in the life around him. We have already seen how hard necessity, as well as certain basic skills, are taught by the laborious work that is the lot of farmboys from an early age. But the scattered small plantations are not entirely isolated; hospitality is a supreme obligation, especially when a household has to mark an event such as a christening, wedding, or funeral. At these and other occasions a youngster learns to relish "company and merriment . . . frolic and dance," community for the moment is most real and immediate, and farm folk get some relief from their heavy toil. Important aspects of what life is all about become apparent to young persons.

We see a group seated around the fire in the hall-parlor of the Jarratts' small wooden house. Cutting from his attentive face to those of the older people in the circle of firelight, we discover the rich traditional worlds of meaning that are opened to little Devereux in the gatherings of family and neighbors. He learns folk ballads simply by listening to them sung—for they are not available in written form.

Reconstructing a scene from Jarratt's recollections, we see him return to his family's place after a few years in the West. Soon his oldest brother, celebrating the return, has "contrived to gather a considerable company of people of different sexes and ages, for the purpose of drinking . . . and dancing." Riding up with Devereux on his borrowed horse, we find a large number of guests. The house is too small for the crowd of people, so some of the activity has been moved into the open. Outdoors we see how tankards of hard cider go briskly round, while "the sound of music and dancing" is heard inside. The film moves on to review other, less family-related celebrations—a harvest feast or barbecue. Here we find all the action outdoors. An amused observer's description tells us where and how to film it. "The company" is "under a large tree," there is "Plenty of Toddy" and "a Fiddle and a Banjo played by two Negroes." "The people are very merry, dancing without either Shoes or Stockings and the Girls without Stays."

Sporting pastimes also are important. We see the young lad learning more about the ways of the world as he willingly

Lessons in cruelty were learned at the violent pastime of cockfighting.

A horse race was a test of nerves for gamblers as well as riders.

accepts the tasks of "preparing gamecocks for a match and main" of cockfighting. We see the aggressive strutting of the fierce little birds and then the sudden death strokes aimed by them as they close in mortal contest. Devereux's commitment, and the keen identification of the spectators with the fighting cocks they bet on, all show us how the boy is learning the proud combative values of the society of white men. It is the same with his other eager sporting involvement. We see how his busy "keeping and exercising race-horses" for his older brother culminates, for that brother, in a headlong rush down a narrow quarter-mile track on the courthouse green. In the reckless jostling that ensues, it is the men as well as the animals that are at risk. (Only wealthy gentlemen could afford the imported thoroughbreds that competed in long-distance "course-racing"; common planters and poorer gentlemen raised Virginia horses to run them in violent quarter-races.)

Sporting events have brought the growing boy into close though still respectful contact with the gentlemen who organize these exciting occasions. Now, at age sixteen, Devereux, who once ran away at the sight of a gentleman in a wig, must, by law, be armed with a musket, a cartridge belt, and powder and shot and attend militia musters under the eyes and the command of just such gentlemen. This occasional army of white men has been an important part of English Virginia society from early days. At first it had been protection against Indians and marauding Spanish ships, but now in the eastern section of the colony it is mainly directed to the maintenance of law and order against possible slave rebellions.

Watching the muster, we see the men falling into line to perform the exercises, each with the best musket he has been

The militia muster taught the participants lessons of authority and obedience, although afterward the officers treated the men to liquor.

21

able to afford, his cartridge belt drawn on over far-from-uniform clothes. He is visibly a farm boy among farmers, all of whom are roughly lined up and inspected by their gentlemen neighbors.

In the sequel to the muster we see how important are the informal ties and the forms of reward by which gentlemen demonstrate their greatness and their right to respect. We see them magnanimously provide a keg of rum to treat the humble farmers who have left the care of their crops to perform their obligation to the public. Thus we see how the bonds of duty, command, and private generosity, put at the service of the community's interest, can establish so much warm sense of warrior loyalty across distinctions of rank that (as one militia captain reported) the men follow him home from the muster and come before his door "and fire Guns in Token of their Gratitude." The captain further recalled that he would then "give them Punch (rum, sugar, lemon, and water) 'til they dispersed." Here our filming permits us to witness a very characteristic colonial Virginia blend of intimacy and inequality. The drinking draws folks together; gratitude for the favor reminds them of social distinctions. Already the grand southern gentlemen—especially the colonels—use their militia ranks like titles of nobility!

Great Houses, Power Houses

When we compared our aerial views of Virginia with a colonial map, we saw how the map was dominated by the plantations of the grand gentry families established at the ships' loading places along the river frontages. Dissolving through an enlarged section of the map or zooming down from an aerial overview, we must now bring our exploring camera in close to survey the kind of community that is to be found in and around one of these grand residences.

A careful panning over a gentleman's great house and its surroundings shows unmistakably that it is the center of a little empire. Switching between closeups of the plantation house and aerial views or map diagrams, we see how the size of the main building and its associated outhouses (often likened to a village) is an indication of the extent of the great man's reach into the social world around him. The house is in direct proportion to the number of slave quarters and white tenant farms that support its magnificence.

The great house dominated its surroundings in the same way that the master wished to assert his will over those who lived on his plantation.
Courtesy, The Metropolitan Museum of Art, gift of Edgar William and Bernice Chrysler Garbisch.

Close focusing shows not only the dimensions but also how the design of the truly great house expresses the authority of its squire. Amid woods and fields and a jumble of slave quarters and outhouses that do not make an orderly total impression stands the mansion house. It, however, is constructed to a strictly ordered and symmetrical design. (For more than fifty years before the Revolution great houses were built following a pattern similar to that of the Governor's Palace in Williamsburg.) The arrangement is of three main parts: the two flanking dependencies give proper emphasis to the more elevated centerpiece that is an emblem of the dignity of the ruler of the house. Built in view of some great inland waterway, this statement of social power is visible for miles.

23

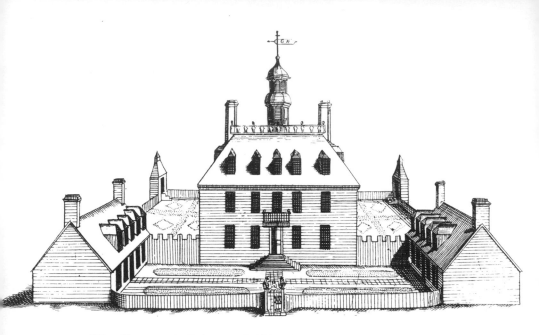

The Governor's Palace at Williamsburg rises above the flanking dependencies that contribute to its show of importance.

Looking closer at life and activities, we see that the great house is in the middle of an important and special kind of old Virginia community. No one is more conscious of this central position than the master. He likes to think of the slaves as his dependents who rely on him to provide for them. "My people," he calls them—sometimes "my family." In this habit he merely makes clear and explicit the patriarchal idea of working relationships that we noticed at the start. To him, the young slave child at the quarter is a distant member of his household. Of course it is clear to us that it is the master and his family who depend on the slaves for both their material support and their social importance.

We begin, therefore, by seeking to know the great house as it is known to Filis. The camera's close-up matches the keen-eyed gaze that the hungry always turn on those who keep a full table and make a lavish display of the opulence that their power gives them. We see also the mockery that is the revenge of the poor as we focus on Filis overhearing many of the less dignified secrets of the great house. There is a constant supply of gossip to the quarter from the personal attendants of the white family. The enjoyment derived from such information is visibly subversive of the exaggerated respect that is required outwardly to be shown to white gentry.

Switching to view the scene through young Devereux's eyes, we recognize that humbler white persons look on the displays at the gentry's "power houses" from a greater distance than do the home plantation slaves. In contrast to Filis's knowledge, the young farm boy's awareness comes from less intimate reports or from an occasional errand. (Even in old age, Devereux Jarratt could never forget the awkwardness of the first time he approached a gentleman and his family at home.) We see him unable to cope with the grandeur of the doorway and the formality of the paneled entrance hall. "I knew not how to introduce myself . . . and what style was proper for accosting persons of their dignity." (Thomas Sutpen, in William Faulkner's great southern novel, *Absalom, Absalom,* was driven throughout his whole life by experiencing such humiliation at the entrance to a Virginia gentleman's great house.)

Viewing and interpreting the confusion of the farm boy introduces into our film some consideration of changing relations between the inhabitants of the little Virginia houses and those for whom the great mansions were built. The common folk face a rising barrier created by increasingly elaborate etiquette among the gentry. Manners were generally rough in the seventeenth century—the first hard decades of English settlement—but during the eighteenth century more and more refined rules of conduct came to distinguish the upper ranks and to make them an exclusive class.

We may best gain a sense of the meaning of this distinction, and of the power that knowledge of etiquette gave within the community, by viewing once again the experiences that taught a child how to know its world. In this case we shall follow a young girl learning to be one of the gentry—to be a lady at home in the great house. Here too surviving documents allow us to follow the actual experiences of a known individual.

Nancy Carter of Nomini Hall, like other daughters of the grand gentry, experienced from earliest years a multiplicity of ways of life. We see her suckled by a slave wet nurse and cared for by the servants. Thus she enters her earliest warm supportive relationships with persons who are so close in their daily lives and yet so different in manner, style, and values from her parents. As she matures, we observe Nancy sometimes drawn voluntarily and sometimes pushed forcibly into the formal style and manners of gentlefolk. She has an increasing sense of being set apart from the slaves. Her awareness of her social rank is further reinforced by the presence about "the Hall" of persons with common folk manners—white servants, craftsmen, and overseers.

We observe both gradual and abrupt lessons—all parts of a continuous training process that is making a lady out of the little girl who was at first used to mixing with slaves and servants. Early on she learns continuously to model herself on her parents and to regard slaves and servants as inferiors whose ways of speaking and acting are to be avoided. The first big reward for such learning is her acceptance, at age ten or eleven, as a person fit to leave the children's room and to sit at the formal dining

During the dancing lesson a young lady learned formal movements that completed her separation from the black folk.

table together with her parents and some of the guests for whom great Virginia gentlemen constantly keep open house.

As Nancy matures, she is increasingly subjected to a more conscious and forceful education in polite manners. At age twelve she must submit in her clothing to the restraints of rigid stays, and she is disciplined in her deportment through dancing lessons. The new demands are very clear in the minuet, quadrille, and other formal steps, where her body movements are trained so that they may not be loose and free (as those of the lower classes are) but rather precise and controlled. We follow as her spirit and sense of decorum and of timing are regulated by constant application to a musical instrument. She is set to learn the guitar. Her mind is shaped and directed to what are defined as higher thoughts—thoughts that elevated these genteel persons above those of common clay. She is taken beyond the three R's into a close attention to the appreciation and imitation of refined writing style. The *Spectator* essays of the English authors, Addison and Steele, are the universally acclaimed model used for this purpose.

The very setting in which Nancy learns these lessons expresses the same ideas. Focusing on the house interior, with flashbacks to earlier times, establishes how the Virginia gentry have used architecture to create highly controlled living spaces—settings for more refined etiquette. The balance and order of the outside appearance of the great mansion is matched by the interior. Each floor of the house is divided by walls lined with fine wooden paneling to create particularized zones— rooms to keep more neatly apart the different operations of living. The specialness of the dining room—a place for table manners—can be sensed from the fact that Nancy has had to graduate from the nursery to be allowed to eat her meals there. Together with the silver and china place settings, each of the high-backed chairs defines a particular social space for every one of those at dinner.

Viewing this arrangement enables our film to demonstrate how furnishings can be combined with architecture to create a highly ordered environment. We nowadays take the separation of living functions into different rooms so much for granted that we do not see anything remarkable in these colonial Georgian houses. But it was quite usual before the eighteenth century, in Europe as well as in America, to find the beds of members of the household prominently placed in parlors and rooms where formal meals were eaten. In the Virginia in which Nancy is growing up, the creation of specialized rooms and of opportunities for privacy in the great houses of the gentry contrasts sharply with the close physical contact and combining of living functions found in the one-room slave cabins and the cramped little houses of the common people.

Of course we must not exaggerate the extent of the controls or the attainment of privacy. Glimpses of daily living reveal that every part of the great house is still very public by our standards; few persons have a room all to themselves—even the parental married couples might have a sleep-in slave close by them. At times of entertainment, feasting, and dancing, the sharing of beds by comparative strangers of the same sex is not at all unusual.

The constraints of polite etiquette are also experienced in moderation compared to the strictness of the Victorian age in which Nancy's grandchildren raised their children. In the years before the Revolution there are more outlets for young ladies to engage in contests and vigorous exertion. Through the eyes of a surprised English visitor watching a colonial high society ball, we see how, "towards the close of an evening," when the company are pretty well tired of formal decorous steps, "it is usual to dance jiggs"—tunes and steps "originally borrowed from the Negroes." We see "a gentleman and lady stand up, and dance about the room, one of them retiring, the other pursuing, then perhaps meeting in an irregular fantastical manner." Evidently we are looking at a clear imitation of bold courtship by both sexes, and we see that the performance is watched keenly by the whole company; their expressions keep the score in what is certainly understood as a contest in this competitive society.

In addition to permitted displays of spirit, a young girl can also stage rebellions. We see Nancy lapse into the unpardonable vulgarity of hair pulling and scratching in a fight with her younger sister over a prize possession. More subtly on another occasion, she uses her new-won accomplishment in polite speech to mouth a sarcastic account of her delinquent brother's conduct. She goads him into a physical attack on her—for which we see him flogged. Through watching all this training we come to understand the pressures on Nancy. We see how she is being taught to place strong restraints on the aggressive impulses she feels, and how she is drawn on by a growing awareness that skill in dancing and dinner table conversation will enhance her social standing. A reputation for accomplishment will be an important addition to her dowry and inheritance in determining her marriage chances—and so her life prospects.

The results of Nancy's training—the scope for achievement that a Virginia gentlewoman might realize—can be viewed directly in the capabilities that we see in her mother, Anne Tasker Carter. The feminine mystique—the expectation that women be continually sunny and generous—is already operating. Mrs. Carter is observed to be "prudent, always cheerful, never without Something pleasant, a remarkable Economist, perfectly acquainted . . . with the good-management of Children, . . . and is also well acquainted . . . with the formality and Ceremony which we find . . . in high Life." We see her about the great house, in charge of a large poultry yard, running a garden and orchard with two gardeners working for her, and managing a vast household where there are always guests. She herself reckoned up that "this Family one year with another, consumes 27000 lb of Pork; and twenty Beeves. 550 Bushels of Wheat. besides corn—4 Hogsheads of Rum, and 150 Gallons of Brandy."

The experience of learning to become one of the gentlefolk is rather different for Nancy's brothers. We see that the steps by which well-born infants learn to avoid the ways of the slaves and common folk and to acquire genteel manners is more prolonged, more complicated, and ultimately less complete for the sons of the great house than was expected to be the case for ladies. Nancy's brothers at Nomini Hall begin also in close relationships to blacks, but *they* continue longer to engage in forms of physical contact with those who are defined as their inferiors. We see this contrast clearly as, with Nancy, we watch her brother Bob, even at age sixteen, fighting "for mere Diversion" with a slave boy.

Nancy is envious as well as contemptuous of her brother and her cousin as they feel free to encourage slaves to bring a fiddle into the schoolhouse so blacks and whites can all dance together. We also see how, with even more mixed emotions concerning his greater freedom, Nancy makes scandal about her eighteen-year-old brother's intimacies with slaves. She promotes the rumor that Ben is the nightwalker who has disturbed everyone in the house by attempting to lie with Sukey, the sixteen-year-old slave girl who sleeps as an attendant in the girls' upstairs room. Clearly the boys' way of life continues to give them such opportunities. As they take up their places of command in society, they will be subtly compelled to hold their own in the rough worlds of field workers, militiamen, race goers, and eventually voters at election time.

Schoolroom scenes show the controls of a tough mental discipline being forced upon the lads. As a particular proof of the manly quality and the vigor of their minds, they have to

Birch rods were the emblem of the schoolmaster; Latin, mathematics, and flogging were intended to toughen the minds of young gentlemen.

learn not just manners, dancing, letters, and refined ways of writing English, but also mathematics and stylish proficiency in an ancient language. We see clearly that knowledge of Latin is the ultimate hallmark of a true gentleman as our camera picks up younger brother Bob applying himself early to this arduous study. He is beginning voluntarily—after he has been told (only partly in jest) "that without he understands Latin, he will never be able to win a young Lady of Family and fashion for his Wife." Gentlemen's sons also have to learn surveying and accounting

and much else besides in the hard school of plantation manage-
ment. They have to be ready for a whipping if they fail or are
considered neglectful and delinquent.

Links to a Larger World

All knowledge is power, but the kind of education given to
sons of gentlemen like Ben and Bob Carter is especially designed to make them assume responsibility and play a com-
manding role in the society of the parishes and counties in
which they live.

Maritime Commerce

Acquaintance with the ways of the big world, combined
with their familiarity with the ways of their neighborhoods,
secured the dominance of the Virginia gentry. Watching Nancy's father, busy with his correspondence, and then following
the letters to their destinations in Williamsburg, Norfolk, and
London reveals how his knowledge of affairs makes him an
indispensable link between the little communities among which

*Often gentlemen-planters
were also merchants who
linked the trade of their
neighborhoods with the
greater society of Vir-
ginia and the Atlantic
world.*

he lives and the greater society of Virginia and the Atlantic world.

Prior to 1730 most trade had been in the hands of substantial planters who corresponded with London merchants. Taking the camera back earlier in time, we see these merchants send ships across the Atlantic and up the rivers to the docks that the large planters maintain on the waterfronts before their houses. We observe leading Virginia gentlemen importing stocks of manufactured goods sufficient not only for their own dependents but also to be able to advance supplies to their less well-connected neighbors. These neighboring small farmers pay for the goods with part of their tobacco crops. Those crops are in turn shipped back in huge barrels called hogsheads to London by the great planters, along with their own, for the merchant to sell on the English market. The merchant takes a commission, deducts the value of the goods he has sent out, and enters in his books whatever balance remains to the credit of his Virginia planter correspondent.

Still directed at the London end of this commerce, the camera shows how the merchant is accustomed to make payments on behalf of his plantation clients when he receives bills of exchange signed by them. These bills are thus the equivalent

Ships like these at Yorktown carried the exports and imports that determined the economic life of the colonial economy. Courtesy, The Mariners' Museum, Newport News, Va.

of modern-day checks, and the English merchants are effectively the bankers for Virginia in the colonial era. Since there are no banks in the colony, only the great planters who operate on a scale to correspond with London have access to the main financial system. The role of these gentlemen as intermediaries is a considerable source of power for them in their own local communities. (By the time of the Revolution, however, the development of company-owned stores, and eventually of banks, has reduced this kind of gentry influence in the countryside.)

Church

The kinds of knowledge that were the preserve of gentlemen gave them an advantage everywhere. At the Sunday service in the parish church we find them able to appreciate the learned sermons that meant much less to the common planters. Indeed, the whole design of the church can be seen to show off the assumed superiority of the gentlefolk.

Filming a gathering outside the parish church on a Sunday, we have to find ways to show (as at the militia muster) the easy mingling of persons that nevertheless preserved clear distinctions of rank. Attendance here is compulsory too; all heads of household are required by law to come to divine service at least once a month. They are fined if they do not. (The Church of England was then a tax-supported established church; it became the independent Protestant Episcopal Church when the Revolution broke its close connection with both England and the state.) In colonial times the parish vestry, a committee of twelve local gentlemen, not only manages church affairs but raises taxes for poor relief.

Opening with an aerial view of the almost townless landscape, we see how the church building—a grand brick structure in a walled yard—stands alone at a crossroads in the center of its parish, surrounded by woods and fields. Then we see the country folk moving there along roads and bridle paths; they assemble well before the appointed hour. The gentry come in carriages, their sons and servants riding escort. Lesser folks come on horseback; slaves (but not many of them) come on foot.

Through the eyes of a visitor from the North, and with the help of his commentary, we observe the animated activities that develop. We see on every hand the "giving and receiving letters of business, reading Advertisements (nailed to the church door), consulting about the price of Tobacco, . . . and settling

The parish church was the largest building most persons in colonial Virginia ever entered.

either the lineage, Age, or qualities of favourite Horses." We see how these engrossing conversations are not easily abandoned. "It is not the Custom for Gentlemen to go into Church til Service is beginning, when they enter in a Body" to take their places right at the front of the church. They are apart from the ladies who are already seated farther back. Farmers and their wives, seated apart, are even farther back. Slaves have had to climb up into a little gallery behind the high pulpit.

Our camera seeks to pick up arrangements and details that will instruct us in the knowledge of themselves and of their world that colonial people had. The camera holds for a moment on the grand doorway arched over with rich colored brick, and then it moves on to convey a sense of the lofty interior. The church is the largest enclosed space that most of the people now at prayer ever enter in their lives.

Inside, our eyes are drawn to significant details such as the royal coat of arms prominent on the farthest wall. Listening in on the service, we hear lessons being taught that match this visual display. Most obviously there are the formal prayers for the king, but we observe also how the occasion itself gives instruction about legitimate authority. The whole arrangement of the house of worship expresses the power of a series of

The commandments on the end wall at Bruton Parish Church in Williamsburg teach duty; the high pulpit demonstrates authority from above.

reigning patriarchs from God downward to the king, the magistrates, and great men of the parish who sit in the foremost seats, and then to the male heads of household who are seated apart from their wives in their own assigned pews.

Immediately after we entered we became aware of the great high pulpit. Now, fastening attention on it, we come to understand it as the strongest statement about how authority descends from on high. It is the official teaching of the church that only a minister, ordained by a bishop in England, can mount up into this high "seat" and interpret the Word of God to the people. The people are appropriately seated below him, arranged in order according to their rank and importance.

The comparatively small number of slaves who come are given a position out of the way in this church. (When they came to organize their own Christian worship, it was not along the lines of the service of the Church of England.) So when we discover Filis in the gallery behind the pulpit, on this Sunday, she is watching the occasion distantly, uninvolved. Young Devereux Jarratt, too, despite his careful instruction in the catechism, finds the service rather incomprehensible. He is seen here, bored, on one of the very few occasions when he attends church.

Following Devereux out of the church and on into his career as a young schoolmaster, we see him caught up in the beginnings of a great popular movement to replace the formal piety of the traditional parish church with vital religion, as it was called—the intense and demanding religion of born-again Christians. Devereux's rejection of the old way and his entrance into the new way is a calling accepted by many of his own and the next generation. (He was unusual only in remaining loyal to the old church while practicing the new piety.) Tracing further his learning experiences introduces us to the popular religious movement that is one of the great revolutions already in progress in Virginia when what we call *the* American Revolution is beginning.

We go to the West with Devereux. He is now, in 1751, a nineteen-year-old optimist who is anxious to escape the drudgeries of farm life by becoming a schoolmaster. We see him fall under the influence of one of those persons who are spreading a new view of what true religion is—"New Lights" they are mockingly called by those who hate and fear them. We watch the lad being drawn into this new piety. In his case it is not through hearing a hellfire preacher but through impressions made on him by a strict life and a solemn, serious manner of

The new evangelical piety stressed family prayers.

behavior. His change of heart begins during regular, devotional reading of the Bible and of sermons written about Scripture texts.

Seeking conversion, Devereux learns to renounce all the pleasurable pastime activities that had been so important to the community of his childhood. On a return visit to his brothers he tries to persuade them that dancing, horse racing, cockfighting, card playing, and all manner of gaming are a worldliness leading to damnation. They must renounce such pleasures, change their ways, and seek God's grace while maintaining a posture of prayer and repentance at all times, night and day. He fails.

Our camera now moves out into the society at large and we can see how many households are making the changes he urges. Large gatherings are attracted by groups of traveling preachers who urge everyone to turn to vital or Gospel religion. These preachers—common men, one of them a black—are raising up a popular movement that links farm folk and slaves to

The revival camp meeting was seen by many at the time of the Revolution as a new and shocking kind of disorder. Courtesy, New-York Historical Society.

the great world in a very different way from the parish church. We observe how stirring are the scenes of awakening, repentance, and conversion that the preachers call forth. From the reaction of bystanders and disrupters—of whom there are many—it appears clear that such scenes (now a very familiar part of the life of the South) are entirely new and shocking to those seeing them for the first time.

Our film here moves on from Devereux Jarratt's experiences to trace the sudden rise of the Baptists in the 1760s. The Methodists gain followers in the same way in the 1770s and '80s. During the very decades that see the revolution against British rule, these two churches, or movements, are growing to greatness and making a revolution in southern religious life. The Virginia Statute for Freedom of Religion and the separation of church and state that follow the Revolution are only part of the alterations that born-again Christianity is bringing about. The customs and the outlook of the people are being deeply changed.

Courthouse

As a center of community organization, the parish church was undermined in late colonial times (and overthrown during the Revolution) by the religious stirrings among the common people in which we have seen young Devereux Jarratt participate. Our camera moves in now on the other main community meeting place of colonial times. The county courthouse gained enhanced importance as a center of local government during the Revolution. It was the administrative as well as the judicial capital of its region; it was the place of elections; and it naturally became the rallying point for assembling the contingents for the armies that were gathered in Virginia to fight the British.

Like the church, the courthouse stands among trees and fields at a crossroads in the middle of the county. There is a tavern nearby, a store, and a little jail. A court day once a month commands very general attendance because it is also the occasion for horse trading, a peddlers' market, and a time for settling debts and circulating news. Inside the courthouse we find the gentleman justices, who are among the county's foremost owners of land and slaves, sitting on a great bench—a raised desk that is set off with fine wooden paneling. Over their heads, a royal coat of arms placed high on the wall proclaims that all the justices do is in the name of the king across the seas. The ceremonials of the court echo this loud statement with the opening and closing "God Save the King" and the solemn swearing of loyalty oaths.

Watching plain men, common planters, preparing their business for the court—proving wills, giving security to pay debts, and so forth—we realize that about one in three of the men do not sign in writing but only make a mark, leaving it to a clerk to set their names down underneath. (Nearly all the farm women do the same, though the total number of women participating is small since in colonial times, and for another century after, men controlled their wives' and daughters' property.)

With the recognition of a high rate of illiteracy and semiliteracy, we can appreciate better as we follow the words and observe the forms of action how the procedures at the courthouse teach these country people most of what they know about government, and (for the whites) about their rights as freeborn subjects of the king. We see how Americans are still strongly committed to the British constitution, which has traditionally been unwritten. Rather than being contained in a single document, it rests on centuries of decisions that were derived from custom.

It is at the courthouse on court day that the special knowledge of the gentlemen contributes most to their domination of their communities. Property—ownership of land and slaves—is the most important fact of social life in old Virginia. Property is strictly regulated by law. But the law is not controlled by highly trained professionals as it will be in our society. The education and experience of the Virginia gentry give them enough knowledge to apply the law to the affairs of themselves and their neighbors.

Five important looking men sit on the bench. They wear periwigs, fine coats, waistcoats, lace collars, and cuffs. They are but a few out of some two dozen gentlemen of the county who have been commissioned as justices of the peace to conduct the local court's business. Usually only about a half-dozen of them act at any one time. Our film must attempt to show how a particular ideal of community is expressed in the system of these courts. The gentlemen of the bench do their work as magistrates without pay, since it is a keenly sought honor to be named by the governor in the king's commission as a "J.P." The roman principle of noblesse oblige demands that gentlemen give service to the public without compensation. In return their office gives them great dignity in county society.

Magistrates' courts are not now considered a major part of the American political system, but as the camera moves in on the work of the county justices in old Virginia we see how important this institution then was, both symbolically and practically. Criminal justice is surrounded by impressive public ceremonies. The public whipping post is in full view; it stands there for white offenders as well as black. Nearby is a gallows, and there is a gibbet with the bones of a rebellious slave whose offense was judged so heinous that he was denied burial in order that his body be a lasting warning to others. No one can grow up without direct knowledge of the awful ceremonial of the public hanging of convicted slaves near the courthouse. (Whites accused of a felony are sent, together with a jury of their neighbors, to Williamsburg for trial—and are executed there if found guilty.)

Following a day in the court, the chief work we see the justices doing is running local government, maintaining land titles, and incessantly regulating debts. The colony has little circulating cash and lives on credit without the aid of credit cards. A tangle of monetary obligations thus connects every household to numerous others as well as to the storekeepers.

All this—which also strengthens the power of the wealthy gentlemen over poorer folk—requires constant supervision by the courts.

The Election

The regular court day is over; our picture fades out as dusk falls on the country folk still drinking and talking business—some dancing to a fiddle and a banjar (an African stringed instrument) played by a couple of blacks outside the ordinary or tavern. As the picture forms again, we find it is another occasion—also at the courthouse—an election day.

Whenever a member of the legislature dies or resigns or when the royal governor decides (sometimes after a long interval) to call a new election, a writ is sent to the sheriff of each county requiring him to appoint a day, conduct a poll, and return the names of one or two men elected to serve as burgesses. (The sheriff, like the justices, is not a salaried official but a leading gentleman of the county performing this and many other services to the public, though he is rewarded by being allowed to keep a percentage of all the debts and taxes he collects.) Attendance at the election is in theory compulsory for all those entitled to vote—that is, any white male over twenty-one years of age who owns one hundred acres without a house or twenty-five with one. But the legal requirement that property owners should vote is not enforced; as we shall see, there are other means to encourage participation.

Polling—the shouting aloud and recording of votes—is a very public affair. The camera zooms in on a long table set up outside the courthouse at which the sheriff sits together with the candidates and the clerks (appointed and paid) by each of them. The voters come to the table and give their names. The sheriff asks for whom they wish to vote, and in front of everyone they have to call aloud their choices. The clerks for those candidates who receive a vote enter on their poll sheet not just a mark but the name of the voter. Clearly honor and personal relationships are very much involved. The candidates express this openly: "Your vote is appreciated," says one. And when we see a man of standing and influence come and declare his vote, the gentleman named exclaims: "I shall treasure that vote in my memory. It will be regarded as a feather in my cap forever."

Shifting our view from the table to negotiations in the tavern or to flashbacks of conversations taking place before the

Candidates who attended an election acknowledged the support of those who gave them their votes in the public polling.

election, we see that voting is not random or arbitrary. Candidates cannot hope to get elected unless they are eminent gentlemen and have the active support of some of the great gentlemen of the county. But the backing of the few great gentlemen can only be effective if it is turned into a multitude of votes. To do this a candidate has to make himself personally agreeable to the voters. This is accomplished in many ways, but we watch it directly confirmed by an ancient practice: the candidates supply barrels of rum to treat the voters.

We follow the campaign of Colonel Edmund Scarburgh. It is reported at an inquiry into his conduct that he had given "strong Liquors to the People . . . once at a Race, and the other Time at a Muster"; on the day of election he caused "strong Liquor to be brought in a Cart, near the Court-house Door." We see many people drinking and one rough farmer in buckskins comes up and says, "Give me a Drink, and I will go and vote for Col. Scarburgh." Custom requires that he be given a drink whether he votes for the supplier of the barrel or not. Witnessing the debates over disputed cases, we learn that treating is really a form of the sacred obligation of hospitality; it is a sign that the candidate knows how to be a great gentleman and has regard for the needs of common men. We see then that these elections are not about parties or policies but about choosing the most admired members of the gentry to assist in the revision and maintenance of the laws. Treating thus seems entirely appropriate. In our film, a forward flash to the Revolutionary years shows the young James Madison arguing that treating should not be continued in the new republic; we see him ignominiously defeated!

There has been much discussion as to whether this electoral system, and similar ones in other American colonies, were democratic or not. For a long time the debate turned on the property qualifications restricting legal exercise of the vote. But lately it has been recognized that the great majority of white heads of household were legally enfranchised—though many showed little interest in availing themselves of their rights. Most historians now believe that attention to the attitudes and practices of the participants is far more important than emphasis on formal legal limitations. Our film presentation of an election will make colonial assumptions about elections understandable: first, because we will see the social setting within which elections take place, and second, because the way the people go about the business of voting will reveal their assumptions about government.

The social setting shown by the camera is a small rural community where the candidates and most of the voters are well known to each other by rank, family background, personal qualities, and mutual obligations. Watching, we are also made aware that the common assumption is that government— whether at the county court level or in the legislature—should be entrusted to the gentry since they are men of property and learning. This assumption arises from the dominance of the gentlemen in every sphere of life. (That dominance is only beginning to be challenged at the end of the colonial era, and that challenge is largely restricted to the sphere of religion.) Observing an election we see that it is free and that campaigning is vigorous. Though the common farmers are subject to all sorts of pressures from the gentlefolk, it appears from their actions and from the way they are addressed that the farmers are recognized to have both the right and the duty to choose whichever of the rival gentleman candidates they consider most fit to be trusted with the making of laws and the guarding of the liberty of all free men. For this liberty both gentlemen and plain folk prove willing in large numbers to sacrifice comfort, property, and even life itself in the course of the Revolutionary War.

Williamsburg

The gentlemen elected as representatives of each county make their way to Williamsburg to attend the legislature whenever they are summoned by the royal governor. The capital town is a special community—the only one of its kind—at the hub of colonial Virginia. A camera carefully directed at Williamsburg shows how ideas about social order, about the ways people should be connected to each other and to the larger world, are expressed in the colonial design of this place. We circle and zoom in on Williamsburg from an aerial overview, observing its layout.

The palace of the king's representative, the governor, is prominently placed facing a long green at the center; near it is the church that is the official place of worship for the governor and all who come to spend any time in the colonial capital. The green on which the church and palace stand bisects the mile-long street that runs from the College of William and Mary to the Capitol, seat of the legislature and the General Court. The College is a part of the colony's government-maintained church. We move in even closer on its fine cluster of buildings. We notice that this place of learning is staffed by clergymen dressed in black gowns and wearing white cravats (Geneva collars) at their necks. Most of them come from the ancient university of Oxford, in the mother country. Their mission is to make English Christian gentlemen out of the sons of the leading families in the colony. Most of the students bring their own slave attendants as well as horses, reminding us, if their defiant, high-spirited behavior does not, that they already consider themselves perfect Virginia gentlemen.

Leading the eye away from the College up the long axis of the town, the camera picks up the elected burgesses going into the Capitol. A series of views of the building (including aerial ones that show the ground plan) enable us to see that the colonial legislature is housed in a bricks and mortar model of the British constitution.

The Capitol is designed and constructed with two wings: one of these belongs to the king and his commissioned offi-

The legislature of the Virginia colony met in the Capitol at Williamsburg.

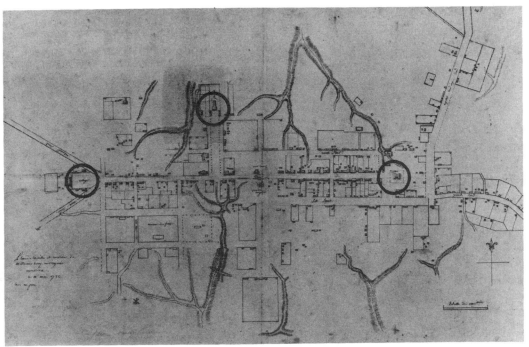

A 1781 map of Williamsburg shows the College (left), the Governor's Palace (upper center), and the Capitol (right).

45

cials—the crown in its executive, judicial, and legislative capacities; the other belongs to the elected representatives of the people. In the first, the western wing, the governor or lieutenant governor sits with the king's Council. This upper house is considered the colonial equivalent of the hereditary body of advisers to the sovereign, the British House of Lords. Opposite them, in the eastern wing, sit the burgesses. They proudly identified themselves with the revered House of Commons, the British legislative body made up of representatives of counties and towns or boroughs. This body was renowned for its centuries-long defense of the rights of the people. The Virginia House of Burgesses—so called because originally Virginia was going to be divided into boroughs—copies most of its own procedures from those of the Commons.

The county representatives are taking their places in the house; proceedings begin. Seeing through the eyes of one of the new burgesses, we recognize that, while the procedures of the legislature are elaborate and modeled closely on those of the English Parliament, much of the work of this colonial legislature is like the familiar business conducted at the courthouses.

The wing where the House of Burgesses met (right) was joined to the wing where the Council and General Court met (left) by the raised center gallery.

Modern bureaucracy has not yet appeared; big government is a long, long way off. The whole colony has only a handful of paid officials, and most of them operate in a decentralized way under the eyes of the county courts.

We watch the burgesses in session as they carry on a county court-style supervision on a colony-wide basis. They are exercising a mixture of legislative, judicial, and administrative authority that seems very strange to us in an age of specialization. To be sure, they make or revise the laws, but they also receive claims for all sorts of compensation—for slaves executed or killed as outlaws, for the trouble of recapturing runaways, for disablement on military service, and so on and on. They receive endless petitions on the adjustment of boundaries, the creation of new counties and parishes, the location of ferries and tobacco inspection warehouses, etc. The needs of local communities—as defined by the dominant white males in them—are very much present to the House of Burgesses and are dealt with by drawing on the experience that nearly all the members have of long service in their counties.

Close observation also reveals how the house is managed by a small group of leading members, most of them wealthy and cultured gentlemen. They are from old families, well established in long-settled counties, yet the observant eye detects that they owe their influence not just to such aristocratic attributes but also to the practical skills gained in managing local affairs. Their fellow legislators rely on them just as the county voters do, reelecting them year after year.

The occasion created by the meeting of the Assembly is not unlike that of a county court day, only with Williamsburg as the courthouse green for the whole colony. Above the household level, colonial Virginia society is a world of occasional community. People live scattered and great importance is attached to the times and places of their coming together—at church, at the racetrack, at the courthouse. Williamsburg repeats this pattern. The population swells from an everyday level of fewer than two thousand people to somewhere between five and six thousand during the "Publick Times" when the General Court and House of Burgesses meet for their spring and fall sessions. Balls and assemblies, races, theatrical performances, fairs, trading of all sorts, and the inevitable gaming in the overflowing taverns make an amazing bustle and congestion that is relished by citizens and traders alike.

But Williamsburg is not merely a trade fair. Here, the leaders of the scattered communities meet. They not only do business with each other but are drawn into closer contact with the fashion and culture of Great Britain. We must show images of the London of the day, intercut with scenes of Williamsburg, to demonstrate how the culture of the metropolis is affecting the life of the little colonial capital, and so the whole of Virginia. The storekeepers use the opportunity created by the periodic gathering of the leaders of Virginia to extend their market for imported luxuries. The local artisans produce imitations of these imports. All of this insures availability in the colonies of novelties—new fashions in carriages, dress, and house furnishings.

By following purchases on to their reception into everyday life in plantation and farmhouses, we see how important the new objects are in providing new images of what life can become. Then we see the book trade and innovations more directly in the realm of the intellect. Merchants and traders everywhere sell Bibles and popular items, but the Printing Office in Williamsburg, with its large stock of volumes, is really the only bookstore in the colony. It sells not only current works on science, medicine, law, and government, but also quantities of a new boom product of the late colonial age—the novel of "sensibility."

Williamsburg stores offered London fashions, and so London ideas.

It would be difficult on film to communicate the way these books encourage those who now read them so avidly to become fascinated by their own emotions, but perhaps it could be done by showing readings aloud and discussion. Somehow we have to indicate the connections between this new preoccupation with self and the new refinement of private living space that we have seen in the design and furnishing of a great house interior. These designs and the equipment to go with them are also being promoted by the stores in town.

As the center of government, Williamsburg exists to preserve and maintain an established order; as a center of commerce and new ideas, it is doing much to alter the world.

A Changing World

We have now had many glimpses of colonial communities and ways of life. We have looked into some of the circumstances that made the variety of persons to be found in colonial Virginia so very different from the variety of persons we see about us nowadays. Viewing those circumstances enables us not only to appreciate the differences but also to begin to understand colonial slaves, farm folk, and gentry as they understood themselves. In our screening of their lives through our cinematic imagination we have also seen signs of change in the colonial world. Those changes are accelerated by the Revolution, but they are already in progress before it, and, indeed, do much to explain why white Virginians and other Americans are ready to assert their independence.

It will be useful to interrupt the film exploration and to take stock of the trends that we have seen altering the experiences of life in colonial Virginia. It will be convenient to make this summing up under four distinct headings:

Consumerism Reinforces Gender and Class Distinctions

The rapidly increasing availability of fancy goods contributed to the spread of polite living. Today, in the aftermath of the alternative culture protest, we feel that there is both a positive and a negative aspect to the advance of refinement. On the positive side, etiquette teaches increased respect for those with whom we interact. It maintains around each person an individual social space into which others are not to intrude. On the negative side, it must be acknowledged that refinement is only achieved by placing everyone's body under repressive controls from a very early age. The effects on the lives of all Americans of that more special individual social space and of those stricter physical restraints is one reason why the increased availability of luxury goods in the later colonial period was so important.

The gentlefolk's fine chairs, the dining tables with individual place settings, and the equipment for eating politely all demanded to be used in ways that required increased self-containment and concern over how one impinged on others—

Women were urged to "Keep Within Compass."

requirements that were reinforced, as we have seen among the most refined, by instruction in music, dancing, and decorum. The goods that indicated a more controlled life-style—simpler chairs and farmhouse tables, for instance—were already coming into fairly general use among whites by the time of the Revolution. Succeeding generations saw the continued advance of that style. There was a steady multiplication of private spaces through the construction of more and more center-passage houses for middling and eventually poorer folk—and after emancipation, for blacks too.

The extension of etiquette and the refined life-style that went with more elaborate furnishings had very important consequences. The innovations reinforced class barriers between those who had learned how to be refined and those who had not. They also gave a special role to women—or at least to those women living within the expanding part of society that was polite. A particular delicacy was attributed to white females, and—as homes came to be secluded centers of refinement—wives and mothers came to be idealized as the angels of the house, entrusted with a special care for domesticity and its restraints.

The Puritanical Revolution in Religion

The restraints of refinement were as nothing to the restrictions imposed by the new morality introduced by the born-again evangelicals. The converts cut their hair short (or wore it tied up severely), they dressed plainly, forbidding themselves any ornaments or jewelry, and they were bound to live soberly and solemnly, renouncing all sports, gaming, frolic, and dance. The Presbyterian and Baptist church meetings and the Methodist classes brought a new kind of ordered community into Virginia as well as establishing a strong mutual discipline among their members. In their great revivalist meetings, however, these strict evangelicals found a blessed release from control into ecstasy—very free and powerful physical expressions of sacred emotion.

Inevitably the apparent absence of restraints in the camp meetings was outrageous to the polite gentlefolk, while the severity of New-Light morals seemed to condemn and to threaten the way of life of all who were not converted. In the years just before the Revolution, there were repeated attempts to suppress the new movement and to break up its great revivalist assemblies. In vain. The Baptists flourished under persecution. In the years after the Revolutionary War, they succeeded, together with the Methodists and Presbyterians, in redefining true Christianity for most white Virginians. When the Episcopal church began in the 1800s to recover from its overthrow, it too was an evangelical religion.

Society Reorganized on a Contract Basis

While the Baptists and other New Lights were turning multitudes to a new conception of religion and morality, white Virginians more generally found they faced the challenge of taxation without representation from the British Parliament. The political leaders of the colony, accustomed to operating under the rule of London, protested in 1764 but would probably have accepted the Stamp Tax as unavoidable when it was imposed in 1765. Richard Henry Lee, subsequently a great patriot, even applied for a job as a tax collector. Suddenly the leaders found a wave of rebellious protest among the ordinary people. This was the wave that carried Patrick Henry and his anti-Stamp Act resolutions to unrivaled popularity. The established leaders learned their lesson; they included Patrick Henry in their number and together organized patriotic vigilance against any further attempts at arbitrary taxation from Great Britain. In short, they embarked on the course that led to the Revolution and independence.

The individual's right was as important to the makers of the republican revolution in politics as the individual's soul was to the preachers who made the evangelical revolution in religion. When independence was declared and the king thereby dethroned, the white men of Virginia saw themselves as free individuals entering into a contract with each other.

The terms of this mutual compact were set out in the constitution of their commonwealth. Society had previously been thought of rather as a great family into which people were placed by God at birth to do their duty as it was assigned to them; now society was thought of more distinctly as a voluntary association entered into by individuals who kept themselves as independent as possible in order to follow their own purposes—to engage in "the pursuit of happiness." Many of these white Virginians, equating happiness, more or less, with economic opportunity, were even at this time moving westward with their slaves, if they had any, to take up free land. There were, however, important limitations to this new idea of the social contract: women were to remain under family government, and were not regarded as independent members of the commonwealth; slaves were far more completely excluded from the self-governing association.

Slave and Free Grow Apart

The blacks were denied effective participation in the consumer and the republican revolution. Without property and not having individual farms and a way of life that promoted individualistic values, they were developing in their little village quarters a distinctive Afro-American culture. This can be seen most clearly in the way they took part—as they did on a large scale—in the evangelical religious revolution. Slaves were welcomed as members of the Baptist and Methodist churches; they produced some preachers and congregations of their own, although they were usually organized in fellowship with the whites. Williamsburg had such a church.

Yet the blacks had a different understanding of the Christian message—its Bible histories of chosen people, bondage, and redemption. They received the message so that it accorded with their own Afro-American way of knowing the world. Whites who used to assume (and often still do) that theirs was the only true knowledge were constantly mystified. They could not understand the distinct, though not less Christian, view of the world that could be glimpsed in the black sermons and spirituals—deep expressions of an Afro-American culture that was just then coming into being. In this way the blacks were having a profound nation forming revolution of their own, but it was gradual and was largely unobserved as it carried the people of the quarters in an opposite direction to that of the individualistic white revolutions in politics and religion.

Seeing the Actions; Knowing the People

A completed tour usually takes us back to where we started. We can now return to the scene at Gloucester Courthouse in April 1776 feeling we know how the filming of it should be directed in order to bring out who the participants were. We can now recognize the gentlemen in the courthouse—the justices and the sheriff—and the soldiers outside—mostly common planters' sons. We know their backgrounds and can fit them into their places in society as they themselves knew that society. We understand more of the importance of the ceremonies of oath-taking in a world where literacy rates were low and so we grasp the special meaning attached to the providential interruption of the ancient customary ritual by the handball played by common soldiers. If we then direct our camera to an event that occurred soon afterward in nearby Williamsburg, we shall be viewing a completed little Revolutionary ceremony that we find we are able to interpret immediately with more confidence. We can film it boldly so as to show how it combined new enthusiasms with now familiar traditional practices.

Revolutionary parades celebrated the new Virginia as an association of contracting free white men.

It was reported in the *Virginia Gazette* that on May 15, 1776, the Fifth Virginia Convention had voted "unanimously, that the delegates appointed to . . . General Congress be instructed to propose that the respectable body TO DECLARE THE UNITED COLONIES FREE AND INDEPENDENT STATES." The report continued:

> In consequence of the above resolution . . . some gentlemen made a handsome collection for the purpose of treating the soldiery, who next day were paraded in Waller's grove (near the Capitol). . . . The resolution being read aloud to the army, the following toasts were given, each of them accompanied by a discharge of the artillery and small arms, and the acclamations of all present:
> 1. The American independent states.
> 2. The Grand Congress of the United States.
> 3. General Washington, and victory to the American arms.
> The UNION FLAG of the American states waved upon the Capitol during the whole of this ceremony, which being ended, the soldiers partook of the refreshment prepared for them . . . , and the evening concluded with illuminations, and other demonstrations of joy.

Zooming in on the action we see the republicanized, revitalized version of the militia active in the parade. The salutes that have replaced displays of loyalty to a distant king declare their new identity; they are no longer colonial Englishmen, they are patriotic Virginian Americans now. Yet many important traditional ways survive: their military formation still arranges common farmers and their sons under the domination of gentlemen officers, just as the old militia had done; the aristocratic obligations of the class that supplies those officers is still acknowledged in the treating as well as in the lighting up of the grand houses of the town to mark the momentous occasion.

Tracking back from the parade, the salutes, the declarations, and the issue of tankards of rum, we can pan over the crowd, recognizing a variety of kinds of individuals. Knowing their different ways has come to make up our understanding of this changing world. We see the wives and daughters of gentlemen, of town artisans, and of small farmers. They are all compelled, as women, to be more or less vicarious participants in this very male celebration of the organization of a social contract among free white men. The blacks are there, but the freedom is not for them. Certainly we will also pick up the solemn faces and sober dress of New-Light Baptists and Methodists. Their conduct is restrained—they are sober in the way they show their pleasure at the advancement of American liberty. Many there, continuing their customary ways—whether white country folk or slaves—dance their joy at the happy occasion before the night of illuminations is over. The Baptists and Methodists forbid themselves this form of rejoicing.

Observing those common celebrations enlarges our understanding of what is happening there. The new nation that is coming into being is committed, in the name of American liberty, to uniting not only colonies with very different pasts, but also varied populations within each of its newly constituted states. The tides of change are rendering the population more, not less, diverse; divisions are increasing. There is the widening gulf between the blacks who are developing a profoundly communal culture and the whites with their increasing individualism; there is the opposition between the strict New Lights and those who persist in the enjoyment of dancing and gaming; and there are already seeds of conflict between southern and northern ways. Over time those differences will be the challenges and ordeals of the American Union and also the source of its cultural creativity and human richness.

Learning to look into the world that first gave rise to that original commitment to union in liberty, seeking knowledge, in the way that the best of filmmaking can convey knowledge of other ways of being and of the forms of domination and exploitation that are too often practiced in the name of liberty, we may make the study of the colonial past serve the highest ends of freedom and human understanding to which the American Revolutionaries committed themselves.

Further Reading

Overviews:

The following works deal in general with colonial Virginia society as it emerged from its seventeenth-century beginnings into maturer form, or as it changed through the period of the Revolution.

Rhys Isaac, *The Transformation of Virginia, 1740–1790* (Chapel Hill, N. C., 1982). The first part surveys the landscape, looking (with the aid of illustrations) at the principal kinds of settlements and places of assembly. It reviews the typical varieties of activity observable at such places—among blacks, farmers, and gentry. The second part interprets the dramatic new forms of action, religious and political, that were profoundly changing this world.

Allan Kulikoff, *Tobacco and Slaves: The Development of Southern Cultures in the Chesapeake, 1680–1800* (Chapel Hill, N. C., 1986). A grand work in the tradition of the "new social history." The book traces, with a great many careful measurements, the emergence of the three great "classes"— gentry, small white farmers, and slaves.

Darrett B. and Anita H. Rutman, *A Place in Time: Middlesex County, Virginia, 1650–1750* (New York, 1984). Based on prodigious computerization of all the records for one locality for a century, this book arrives at a brief, clear account of how the rural society of eighteenth-century Virginia took shape. It is rich in human episodes, intuitively interpreted.

Family and home cultures:

Herbert G. Gutman, *The Black Family in Slavery and Freedom, 1750–1925* (New York, 1976). This book looks much wider in time and place than eighteenth-century Virginia, yet it is indispensable for its demonstration of the extent of the black triumph in creating and sustaining families under a system of slavery that denied them the right to do so.

Lawrence W. Levine, *Black Culture and Black Consciousness: Afro-American Folk Thought from Slavery to Freedom* (New York, 1977). A wonderful book of wide scope whose first chapters on the period of slavery provide a compelling view of the way of life of black people in their plantation communities through an interpretation of their forms of group self-expression.

Jan Lewis, *The Pursuit of Happiness: Family and Values in Jefferson's Virginia* (Cambridge, 1983). A finely written book, rich in original sources; it traces the changes from a controlled formality of relationship in the mid-eighteenth century to a seemingly unrestrained sentimentalism in domestic life among the gentry by the early nineteenth century.

Edmund S. Morgan, *Virginians at Home: Family Life in the Eighteenth Century* (Williamsburg, Va., 1952). A short, readable book that pioneered this field and so does not contain the results of recent research.

T. H. Breen, *Tobacco Culture: The Mentality of the Great Tidewater Planters on the Eve of Revolution* (Princeton, N. J., 1985). A short book that deals with the close identification of the gentlemen planters with agriculture and shows the difficulties they experienced with the British merchants, preparing them for Revolution.

Community Politics:

Charles S. Sydnor, *Gentlemen Freeholders: Political Life in Washington's Virginia* (Chapel Hill, N. C., 1952), reissued as *American Revolutionaries in the Making: Political Practices in Washington's Virginia* (New York, 1965). A vivid description of the style of elections and of legislatures, showing the blend of local concerns and larger issues.

Religion:

Donald G. Mathews, *Religion in the Old South* (Chicago, 1977). An excellent brief, clear, and sensitive outline of the revolution in southern worship and morality through the eighteenth century and beyond.

Consumer Revolution:

James Deetz, *In Small Things Forgotten: The Archaeology of Early American Life* (Garden City, N. Y., 1977). Only parts of this little book deal with Virginia, but the whole brilliantly shows how new kinds of imported commodities and designs were changing America.

Eyewitness Accounts:

Hunter Dickinson Farish, ed., *The Journal & Letters of Philip Vickers Fithian, 1773–1774: A Plantation Tutor of the Old Dominion* (Williamsburg, Va., 1965). The diarist, from New Jersey, was close enough to Virginians to learn to understand them and yet distant enough to want to describe their strange ways; a most compelling portrait of life in a plantation house resulted.

Devereux Jarratt, *The Life of the Reverend Devereux Jarratt* (Baltimore, 1806, reprinted, New York, 1969). Also reprinted in part as "The Autobiography of the Reverend Devereux Jarratt, 1732–1763," edited with valuable notes by Douglass Adair, *William and Mary Quarterly*, 3rd Ser., IX (1952), pp. 346–393.

Edward Miles Riley, ed., *The Journal of John Harrower: An Indentured Servant in the Colony of Virginia, 1773–1776* (Williamsburg, Va., 1963). The diary of another tutor—this one a poor Scotsman whose journey and experiences poignantly reveal connections between the Old and the New World, as well as illuminating household life in Virginia.